ARTICLULATION

ARTICULATION

poems by Timothy Kelly

Lynx House Press
Portland, Oregon/Amherst, Massachusetts

Acknowledgements

Some of the poems in this volume first appeared in periodicals as follows:

Stripped: "Clasp," "New Music"
Field: "Works in Olympia WA," "Red Radish," "Three Movements from
    Tai Chi Chuan," "Chinese Finger Trap," "Does Enough Happen,"
    "Two Special Senses," "Closed Head Injury."
Nimrod: "Will This Change?"

Design by Christopher Howell
Cover Art: *Decorative Touches,*
    13" by 13" Embroidery on Velvet, Mixed Fibers
    by Tom Lundberg

Library of Congress Cataloging-in-Publication Data

Kelly, Timothy 1951-
    Articulation : Poems by / Timothy Kelly.
        p. cm.
        ISBN 0-89924-085-2 (cloth) : $18.50 — ISBN 0-89924-084-4
    (paper) : $9.50
        I. Title.
        PS3561.E39719A78 1993
    811'.54—dc20   93-26569
                                                                      CIP

The author wishes to express his gratitude to the King County Arts
Commission, Seattle, for awarding him its 1992 Publication Award.

Lynx House Press
9305 SE Salmon Ct.
Portland, Oregon 97216

        and

Box 640
Amherst, Massachusetts 01002

Lynx House Press books are distributed by Small Press Distribution,
1814 San Pablo Avenue, Berkeley, CA 94702.

for Lisa, Cole and Emmett

Contents

III. Will This Change

I.

Does Enough Happen

DOES ENOUGH HAPPEN?

Gnats spin down pricking
the tensed, emerald lens
of this tarn. For the hour,
trout strike, flashing,
and weave away.

All this water's
parted, day by day,
from sky, now tilting
so suddenly and unreasonably
clear. The few
winnowed clouds maneuver,
gilt by the sun
in decline. Why

is it so hard
to hold the mind
still? At one end,
the outlet tips glassy
over a length of log,
begins its effortless,

ratcheting fall
from one conclusion
to the next.

THREE MOVEMENTS FROM TAI CHI CHUAN

1. *White Stork Cools His Wings*

Stork's wings fan
like the scalloped hand you can't believe
you've drawn. You ante

and yawn, exposing yourself, certainly.

Stork cocks his head
as the wings fold.
Someone has left the glowing
refrigerator standing
wide open.

2. Repulsing the Monkey

What's war? Who remembers?
Class camping in the boiler room?
Canned milk? Clammy cots? Hey.
In my apartment parking lot I dance;
I hold the ball, the trimmed wheel,
the hoop monkey cannot penetrate.
It's tonic; stalking monkey's
batted away.
To him, one day's
like the next. He stretches, yawns,
sits and is still. You say Good monkey, oh
good monkey, easy monkey, no monkey, NO

3. Wave Hands Like Clouds

Fending deadheads, fending snags,
I strained through the fog for channel markers
and called the bearings back. My father, invisible,
adjusted us. No sunrise, no lighthouse cut that air,
but the harbor buoys did finally, clanging.

He knew the harbor and throttled up. I was satisfied.
I lay back in the prow, bundled, and watched
the ceiling glide by. Like being wheeled to surgery
I thought, on a high, silent cart. I remembered
myself walleyed in the snapping sheets, the ether
dripped on gauze, popping lights, sweetness. A face

is rising through green water, rising at me through
the floors of a tall, white house: my head's lifted,
banged down. We're out of the harbor, into open lake,
chop.

CLOSED HEAD INJURY

Big wigs of flowers in every room we wheel by. She
had big red flowers in her blouse that night, and cold rain
running up his arm as he throttled down for gravel.
He ran out because she had been asking him to

get her something. What it was was here a minute ago,
if I would just park him here in peace and let him
think, instead of dicking him around like some little pony.
What it was was her blouse was open and she wanted him

to get her something important. He'd go and be right
back, but now they tie this stinking poodle in a sling
around his neck every morning, this hand I want him to bear
weight on, this hand he won't look at or acknowledge, this

hand they grafted on, he thinks, while he teetered his week
with burrholes ventilating his head, to this dream of reaching
into flowers, a slur of red flowers he was watching rain
wash, a long time, very slowly, off pavement.

THE RECEPTIVE

Bend down, silo,
in this day-dimming
rain, I want to hear
your deepest thoughts run
again. Was it dreaming

that transit, as I walked
the tracks out of Vermilion
childless, sprung,
wanting nothing, worrying
nothing, drawn on
on a sea of undulant corn
and crows. Freight

blew by, missed me.
But the curving chain
of coal- and boxcars
hammered home the same
point and hammered home
the same, and hammered home
the same point again:
music rules

the spheres and
silos and the staggering
spaces between worthwhile
thought. It bathes
the interstices, I thought,
and the thought galvanized me,
the way they will,
drummed up, concussive,
opportunistic, gone.

NEW MUSIC

The road is straight,
the plains are Great, and
on the airwaves, bent, grating
noises, like fizzling bottle rockets
serenade me. University station,
must be.

Hard to hear new music.
Hard to let that meandering dentist
work. Hard, too, to stand too pat
in the well of the tried and true;
yo go there for comfort,
for order, for ease; over and over,
dominant topples tonic, step one two,
step. Meanwhile, out on the wire,
birds pipe random quarter tones.
They look at you looking, and fall
silent. That's odd.

THREE BONY LANDMARKS

1. Pelvis

Here is the cradle that rocks
the ship that girdles the hive
and the honey

And here is the turtle flipped
onto his back; he's got four legs,
and then hasn't any!

See how those chimneystones rise
from the wings? Matisse saw that line
in his dove

And finally our own heads, oblong
and rose, squeezed through with a grace
from above.

2. Rib Cage

Harrow, barrel stave, whale's
curved comb, needles drawn
from the back of a perch: who
canvassed you over, who's
pounding the drum? My father's

friends sit, hands folded, fingers
laced. Are they protecting some
bankable cards? Or has each
corralled some insect?

Outside, the sky's spokes arch
across the lake; inside, black
radish rests on the sinktop;
in weather, the house moves around it
gracefully, turning aside the hail,
batting away dogs.

3. Skull

I kiss
the only house you're sure
to die in, vaulted,
longsuffering, hardbitten
nut. Nodding,

the steer's head's
unearthed, all burlap,
steam, herbs; it's cracked
and the spoons fly at it.
You fall
          down stairs.
Welts are raised there,
a kind of relief
to be read
by fingertip, like the sutures
formed as the fontenels
fuse.

On its bowed stem
your head ripens,
sways like a swallow
on a rush. Lanterns bob.
Classed by volume,
addressed by a dithering
Dane, its expression
accommodates each
insult, unchanged.

TRILLIUM

After a winter of hardening argument
and escalating surgical strikes,
we tramp in the woods and there
find trillium. Were you aware,
she asked, that as they age, they pink?
I wasn't, I said, but knew, as she did,
that pilgrims in the woods were often met
by signs and ciphers slyly disguised
and passed them, consequentially. So
though we were chill in the drizzle
and not yet halfway, we stopped
by that arrangement and ate,
listening to water run wide around us,
and knowing morels, skunk cabbage, and
the whole, slow wash of spring's greening,
of abundance and renewal, would reach,
and float, and with luck dull that jagged
thing harming us. They were beacons
in that monochrome, I thought, glinting
like knives in a galvanized tub. She,
however, saw her cousins in Catawba,
spread out in the woods with flashlights,
searching for walked-off Mad
who wandered, once-a-summer, out
of the circle of cabins, eyes wide, zombiefied,
driven like a spaceship into the mosquitoey dark
by the dream you were supposed to step into
firmly, but were forbidden to startle her from.

OYSTERMEN

Strange flowers, these,
like the collected porcelains my grandmother
threw down the stairs. We set

our lanterns in the beds
and stoop, rain running up the back.
We work until the blanketing tide
tips back over and herons set down
behind us.

You have to love it. Every day
a reckoning: the house torn open,
repeatedly dropped back; the tenants,
like kings at a coup, grey, naked,
gripping their thrones.

WORKS IN OLYMPIA, WA

You have an oyster and your knife is in it
and the trees shiver and the clouds move
behind them and still it does not yield.
It's like talking to Alma, whose brain is bruised.
For days at work I ask Alma who I am, but
she can't remember. I prompt. Earl and I
ate breakfast, she says, meaning her left arm.
She's surrounded by a terrific denseness,
a thwart; she's calling home and the phone's
disconnected and it's not, it's just
not a dream. I handle Earl. I make her
handle Earl, and gradually she learns. It's work.
They're stubborn and they turn away, but they do,
with bitterness and a strange consistency, yield.

SNAPSHOT OF THEM ENSHRINED
ABOVE MY DESK AT WORK

She's drawn him in, wrapped him up,
and he's, for once, allowing it.
He beams back at the camera, full of
himself, his face untroubled, gaze
direct, eyes poised for a slant
into mischief. It was March at Staircase,
the flumed Skokomish falling
pell-mell past us. It dominates
the backdrop, so whisked-white and full
of glancing contradictions, it might
as easily be sky.

I will come in sometimes, after sitting
through a patient's obtuse, interminable
accounting of pain unmoved, and be struck
seeing them, by a fear so quick
it stutters me. I think of Mushim
on her cushion at Green Gulch, sitting
zazen in the chill dojo, 5 a.m., breath
rising, year after year. How could I
have let them get so close to that river?

RIDING THE T IN BOSTON, I REALIZE I'M THE ONLY ONE IN MY CAR NOT LISTENING TO A SONY WALKMAN

I speak of making love last night
in Mikey's front room in Brookline
with Mikey and Sarah and Shanti and Cole
all asleep in adjacent rooms, and how
every time we hit a certain rhythm
the bed began to hop, and how it got
funnier with each shushed position change
until we lie there, still joined, unable
to finish or look at one another, laughing
the harder for not being able to
laugh out loud.

        Salome's wild dance
for Herod won her the Baptist's head
in a dish. She carried it then, slowly
through the house to her mother, past
rows of staring servants, who canted
their heads carefully, from that day
forward, to avoid the withering trial
of having to look her straight in the eye.

SKIN

Gatekeeper, envelope, investment,
scout, I can barely contain myself.
After I get a history, and reach
for the offending knee, everything
I learn's told me by you, by fingertip,
by meandering exploration, and mute.
Touch with intelligence reassures,
always, slows the heart so gingerly clocked
at the instep. Seeing's not believing,

but touch is; it binds
the newborn, haunts the amputee,
speaks the whole truth
after your lover has spoken.

ARTICULATION

I bend to where the levers link, limb
bends, bone ends hinge or pivot eccentric;
it's my job
            to disinhibit this motion, this
flawed translation of will into world.

She is Hmong; her car flipped end
over end, months ago, on the freeway,
in rain. I say put your foot
on a soup can; roll it slowly back
and forth; this row of dice-shaped bones
you broke is still too stiff, needs bending;
this should help.

She translates for her husband, who
was the driver and walked away unscathed.
He comes daily, sits, and watches us work.
They exchange short, sharp sentences;
he shrugs and scowls. The gesture
is unreadable, somehow hostile, trivializing,
it seems to me, her lameness. He looks,
for the first time, at me, and says Soup can?
I say slowly, despite myself, Regular
soup can. Bean can, vegetable can. Any
medium-sized, round steel can. Unopened. Can.

SO

So the gift you didn't know enough
Greek to say no to, the wet sack of smelt
slowly sagging in your lap gave way
by Estelle, fish spilling silver
through splits in the bag. And you,
with nothing else to put them in,
watched them skid, staring, an hour
in the aisle, the bus pitching regularly
off the shoulder, each woman, as she rose
to leave, adjusting her shawl,
dropping one or two back in your lap
as she passed. That

was the week before you fell, gashed
your hand and lost your senses, wobbling
back to the blinding, whitewashed town,
your disinfected, bedless, zen-empty room.
That time, I know, you make it back

for your sister's wedding in Vermilion,
where we took LSD and scuffed confettis
at the edge of the dancefloor a long time
before we could talk. And in no time,
strange, tuxedoed couples all around us
doing the hokey-pokey and you turn
yourself around. That's

what it's all about.

28

FORCED BULBS

Paperwhites rocket
out of a bowl of black stones,
sweet, still sentries centered
in this house's hurricane turning.

Are they alive, exactly?
When they swoon, in a week,
are they saved? I remember barging
headlong into lovemaking one summer
in an empty boathouse in Huron,
scrambling for cover from
a black, drilling hailstorm.
And though I turned on my heel
and flew back out, stung blind and breathless,
I can still see, to this day, those
strained and shining faces.

Rapture's rare enough in life;
is witnessing rapture rarer?
Glimpsed serendipitous, it rings
in relays, reverberating around
the city like Angelus bells,
alerting all to the disposition
of the day, the day divided
by convention, the day filled
with memorable temptations,
capitulations, endless
unanswerable gifts.

II.
Clasp

BUTLER'S *LIVES OF THE SAINTS*

1. Saints' Mothers

Oh yes, they wanted saints,
but forgot the wanting meant
murder, usually, in flowering youth,
usually, arriving on the heels of some
short string of miracles. Oh yes,
they grieved a bit themselves for having
wanted, even Christ's mother, descending
Golgotha, rent by the seventh of
Simeon's swords, wept and doubted,
crying How, Child? and Why?

2. St. Sebastian

Beatific porcupine, bristling arrows,
patron of the archers who left you pierced
for dead, Butler's *Lives of the Saints* tells me
that this cruel volley failed to kill you;
that some good woman gathered you, bound
your wounds, nursed you back to strength sufficient
to see you, months later, climb a parapet
and denounce, loudly, the sins of the Roman governor
as he passed.
             This part of the story
was news to me, who had thought of you only
with hands bound, eyes imploring, bloody shafts like broken spokes
carouseled round your trunk. Of course,
you were right to do it, to lay months
at her hearth, taking broth, festering, delirious,
blue-black, bloated.
                According to Butler, they
dragged you down and crushed your head with stones
right there, so the furious governor might be
fully appraised of your martyr's death. But you
were right. Surely God's exhortation has always been
to speak out from on high against sin,
getting in not the last word, but the best,
giving the philistines pause
                   for one disorienting
moment, one incriminating beat, before,
recovering their indignant senses, they begin
to circle you, palming roadside stones.

3. Hagiography

The monks at Pechory, it was said,
welcomed the blitzing Nazis who tacked
antennae to the onion domes and promised
respite from the rant of the Bolsheviks;
three years later, with Pskov leveled
and half Leningrad starved to death,
the antennae were swept away, and Pechory
closed its walls, once again, to all
but the dwindling faithful.
                              Now this:
twenty glinting onion domes soar above
the walls, five more turquoise, spattered
with stars. Inside, though it's winter,
everything's tidy, swept, well-clipped,
washed. Scowling monks pass, reading
breviary. And reliably, at each turn
in the path, small mosaics or gilt icons
of saints, Christ, or the Virgin, each
with its peculiarly disturbing, sunken, Russian
gaze.
        It's a visited look I realize
I've seen once before, watching mothers
deliver their spastic, protesting children,
morning after morning, to therapy. It's
a wisdom which deranges instead of pacifies,
which hardens and humanizes, both at once.
It's a look I see cultivated carefully,
in these young passing monks.

The faithful,
it's said, are swelling in numbers, and indeed,
by mid-Mass, parishioners are overflowing
out the main doors, standing tiptoe to peer
into the sacristy. They've sacrificed
something, each, to be here. I'm invisible,
inconsequential. The strange language, the cold,
oddly-pitched singing echoes out into
the darkening afternoon. The tour bus revs.
It begins snowing.

SMOKESTACK LIGHTNING

Woody's widowed sister wanted
men around her girls; so for a year,
we were it. We'd drive down to Ashland
late Fridays, and go straight into beers
and rambling. She worked us hard Saturdays,
ticking off chores, commanding the kitchen,
smacking us around like dimwit cattle, insulting
our penned-in, mole-bitten, adolescent lives.

She taught music, doggedly dragging out
her scratchy, overblown classics; we brought down
rock for the girls. One week, after she'd had us
redo the lightning rods on her chimneys
and barn peaks, we brought down the immortal
Smokestack Lightning by the Yardbirds, and
she settled back game, listening hard and scowling
uncomprehendingly, genuinely and hopelessly out of it.

We drank hard and late Saturday nights.
She wanted, she made clear, an artist next,
someone with fine hands, someone capable
of being a lightning rod, a conduit,
of bringing something down from the heavens
to this sad, starved-out earth. We looked
at each other gravely, and nodded. A year later,
she was engaged to a contractor, driving

the girls south to Marysville Sundays, playing
organ in his church. We stopped going down.
Woody asked her though, one time, whether
this hack was an artist, and she looked at him
the way you look at dense, honking relatives
backing slowly into traffic, your wave flagging,
brightness stiffening, and a bonier, more bewildered
look hardening, like scouring weather, in its place.

CHINESE FINGER TRAP

Something of the yoke the ox's head
fits through, of lobster and crab-
traps, of slender checkvalves in the veins
of legs. As you stoop for apples,
the yellowjackets bumble, and you see
the groundhole they fly to.
                              Going in,
coming out, who was it you bumped into
in the middle of the woven tunnel?

Was it the strange cousin you bashed
heads with years ago in the Hay-Maze?
You saw stars and told him to back out
because you had many people behind you.
And he was crying too, and said
the same thing.

TWO SPECIAL SENSES

1. Proprioception

At night, when we fly,
this is the sense insurgent, the instrument
panel tilted and lit, the offshore voice
insisting we're gliding steadily over the house,
that a slow, steady turn of the head
will take us out, over large animals, necks bent,
drinking from a river, nearby; that a nod
will take us down to the salmon frantically
shouldering upstream, splitting the swirled surfaces
with leaps. With waking,

with day, each joint, each articulation
broadcasts a continuous accounting
of its attitude, configuration, position
in space. Summed, by instant, they configure
you, they inform your self-portrait, they orient
and apprise you of your current standing
in the world. Is your elbow bent now? I ask Gina,

head-injured, as she slouches in the bars;
Head straight? Yes, she says, and Yes, so
we bring a mirror, which she curses.
Six months later, after discharge, we've
arranged lunch, and she sweeps into the restaurant
spike-heeled, hair grown out, scars invisible,
so completely put back together I fail,
for a full embarrassing beat, to recognize her.

When she takes my hand, she gives me, slowly,
her gorgeous, leveling, lopsided smile;
she says Your mouth is open.

2. Stereognosis

You do it by hand, this,
by gradual appreciation of surfaces,
outline, heft; by holding a thing,
by caress, you commit it
to memory and can call it back,
tactile, whole, always.

When this fine sense is lost,
though touch is undiminished,
eyes will name commonplaces, but
without conviction. The man,
blindfolded, given an ice cube, says
it's cold, it's square, it
has edges, but

he cannot tell you what it is.
Like love, then. In my dream
of digging potatoes, I uncover you
and glance around, irritated.
I was not expecting to see you here,
I almost say. Then,

more myself, turn and dig again,
refusing to speak altogether.

GAIT CYCLE

1.

Rising to standing
to walking to stairs, these
tell me a story more raveled
than fiction. Among the lame
and halt, gait is a signature
more fluorescent, more fundamental
than any short slash of handwriting
could ever be. Their grace
has been fractured. They labor,
with bent carriages, before
a riveted world. Working
alongside them, I glimpse myself,
eventually.

Movement, in this life, is sign-
language; it paints, prejudices;
coming into a crowded room,
it speaks long
before anything else can.

2.

By convention, the midfoot is yielding,
slightly inverted at heelstrike
to conform to the odd, unpredictable
world; stays loose as the foot comes
to flat, bearing fully now the weight
of the subject and whatever burdens
she bears.
          Then, the process reverses,
the shin rotating outward, the foot stiffening,
so that the surge, travelling visibly,
pelvis, thigh, line of leg, is translated
efficiently into the radiused, circuit-making
earth, and the subject, rising and leaning,
is levered some meager half-yard forward,
another step closer to her presumably
desired end.

3.

The ball arcs off the horizon
like a series of Muybridge snapshots,
and with each, I adjust my route
to close. Something deeply remembered,
deeply pleasuring about tracking
a falling object from on high. Uncompensated,

it took my eyes years to learn this,
circling eccentrically under seasons
of misjudged flies. It chagrined my father,
who tutored, dissected, and gradually,
bewildered, steered clear. Now,

when it works, I cross a great expanse
of field looking up, legs driving,
and may actually leave the earth briefly,
arms out, body extended, to arrest
the long trajectory. If the thing
can be reached, stopped, taken in, and
personal injury, on the crashing return,
averted, I am still, to this day,
amazed, and for that fleeting,
rapturous moment, want nothing more
than to get up, toss it back and be tried again.

4.

Ten months
he teeters and sways.
One wonders, watching this
grudging singlemindedness,
just how ferocious the need
to rise up towering, free
all props, and walk. If
he were twenty years older,
he might be dancing, very high,
very tired, but still out there,
still up. I miss those nights.

At work, I will reach
for a wavering hand, bid
the patient rise. It is very
like a dance sometimes,
a very slow, very deranged
dance. We stand
in a loose embrace, face
to face, moving little,
chatting unhurriedly about what
we've just accomplished
and what we might try next.

5.

Benedictine monks, St. Martin College,
Lacey WA.

I'm thinking of the funeral
of the handsome young priest
who circled my school every morning,
1964, head down, lips moving, obliviously
reading his daily office. I served

that sad, solemn-high, midmorning Mass,
holding the billowing censer's chain
for the bishop's senile
hieroglyphic march. He tripped, too,

at communion, the circle
of concelebrants closing quickly,
arms and murmurs, preventing
his fall. Think with me, briefly,

of human locomotion as a controlled
fall, the freed foot flying forward
just in time, to arrest uprushing
disaster. And these monks,
circling the green below,

corroborate: the body's husk, vessel,
convenience, conveyance, locked
in its mortal spiral. Yet I note
how unswervingly one foot's placed

ahead of the next, even while
their attention's fully given
to their palmed breviary texts.
They move through consecrated space,
steering corrupt bodies toward grace.

I pray lofty thoughts, thoughts
of immanence and service animate me
at my last, but it's the animation
I'll count on, the hand shooting out,
probably bewildered, to gasp

some steadier hand, some last pillar
in this fleshy, sliding, hallucinated world.

LINES AROUND THE EYES

If to hummingbirds we appear
motionless; if simple touching
will varnish the rosewood rail;
if every downed cedar's a city aswarm
with fierce, channeling beetles, then
yes, you look older, yes.
                         In Ohio,
our first August, we hiked in
over fences to a wild quarry,
stripped, swam, stretched out, slept; and
later, climbing out, stopped once more
to fix that scene clearly: weather
had blunted the limestone, opened it;
but the lake nested there
was a black fathom, and glinty.

NUDES

The light thrown off
as you shifted foot
to foot against barnwood; or
my penis' shadow
across my thigh. We talked
about voluptuous nudes,
Modiglianis, our clothes
stretched across a bush
nearby. Talked weather,
sea-changes, battery, love;
I remember that conversation
and the pattern on your cheeks
as you stood up shining,
broadbacked, dry.

THE BLUE HOLE, CASTALIA, OH

1.

The tank's face's glossy and checked
with leaves, the water an algaed murk;
it may, they say, be bottomless, and I
can feature the lost team sailing downward
peacefully now, the farmer and wagon
behind them, having plowed in in 1901
and fallen since. I think of the miles
out of the way, the steep fee paid
to witness another spectacle of absolutely
surpassing plainness; and of other money
I paid years ago to see my next-door
neighbor, whose brother had transformed him
into the Wild Man of Garnett Woods,
captive, in his underwear, in a refrigerator
crate. And how when I said That's your
brother, not a Wild Man, he said I don't
have a brother. That's a Wild Man.

2.

We buy our Blue Hole insulated mugs
and squirrel them back to the car, set them
on the dash side by side, the way we always
pictured ourselves, only half-joking,
ensconced on some farmhouse porch, gone
silvery, rocking. And this, we knew,
against the grave and escalating odds
of catastrophe, visitation, disruption,
change.
       I think of this seeing you nod,
still, to the steaming Blue Hole mug,
your lit face moony, the sleep still in it,
the mystery never less for its proximity, its
constancy, its suspension, daily, before me
inviting song, inviting scrutiny.

CLASP

Tortoise-shell barrette
passes through and bites,
cinching the muscular coil
up off her neck and out
of the bath she's in now
with Cole. She can do it
with one hand. He shouts

like a pitchman here, loving
the reverberations. She shouts
counterpoint; they huddle,
conspire, explode. From
my perch, I can count
her vertebrae, the long,
strong curve of her neck
and back. He dunks. She
reaches a hand back carelessly
to check the clasp, and I

am struck: here is
the gesture that holds
the family together, unconscious,
emblematic, resonant
as a recurring dream, or
the yardful of whitewashed
boulders our old neighbor
mowed around in Cleveland
for years, before I finally
figured out they were arranged
to say Jesus Christ to spacecraft.

III.

Will This Change

REVERBERATING CIRCUITS

1.

I was studying memory, neuroanatomy, cortical mapping
and Nabokov, sped-out, sleep-deprived, slipping and
dying to see whether I'd made an impression
on you. When you showed, I set to your request,

Earl Gray, and we sat up talking, babbling me mostly,
about the cascade of neurotransmitters,
the broad physical storage of memory, circuits
of critical information kept primed, reverberating.

You talked, as I recall, about Van Gogh's
Fourteen Sunflowers; how, seeing them in Amsterdam,
you felt like you knew them, recognized them,
more real than the real ones seem, you said,

and that stopped me just long enough
to realize I'd stopped breathing and was about,
after great wandering, to be kissed. I remember, still,
every detail of that long and glistening night, just

as I'm brought back, unfailingly, smelling boiled cabbage,
to my grandmother's crowded, whistling, zinc-topped
kitchen. Memory's like that, shining through
the new with like patterns, like scraps, farfetched, odd,

but instructive likeness. Why is it, then,
that I learn so poorly so much of what I repeatedly
struggle to, and come back so vividly to so much I never
intended to keep? And who is it tells me, glimmering,

what's about to happen just before it does, or solves
the blocked puzzle two days after I've given it, utterly, up?

2.

Not so much a newsreel
as a diorama, shot fully-formed
before you, compressed, fine-boned,
psychedelically, and for once, finally,
wholly comprehensible. A feeling
of peace and relief obtains,
apparently, despite the hovering sight,
only mildly fascinating, of the medics
sliding your body, birth-bloody, out
of the wreck. No

thank you, keep it all
except for the house of memory, confirmed
and exploded: everything heard, everything
ever seen, processed and retrievable
after all, thrown up at the last
in one almighty, dilated surge.

Do you remember the circus in Moscow?
The sweetness in the face of the clown
who mimed his heartbreaking aria,
eyes locked into ours, then
buried us in flowers, fresh flowers
shooting endlessly out of lapels, collar,
sleeves? We cried then, and harder
the harder the crowd laughed and clapped,
cried in the midst of laughter, revelry,
fanfares, backslaps, hurrahs.

PURSUIT OF WEALTH

He's trying hard to kick me, kick loose
from me, because he's seen the needle
glint. And the penetrating wail that comes,
as he's finally stilled and stuck accuses me
of a betrayal, a coercion so fundamental,
I find myself, for a guilty second
pierced too, weak-kneed, ready to fall
and beg the struggling victim's forgiveness.

Ten minutes, this terrible rift's forgotten.
But, driving home, I begin to see
Charlie Clemens' photos of the bloody
kitchen table which served as his operating suite
in Guazapa, Salvador, six years ago.
My taxes paid, still pay, for nail-filled,
amputating, anti-personnel bombs which maim
primarily children, who wander too far
from bunkers, lost in play. I have tried,
for years, to digest this, transform it,

but it is insoluble. He mentioned anaesthesia;
he often had none. Friends held friends'
children down and sang to them while he cut,
I think he said, sang to them.

DUSK

Another day.
I imagine not loving you
secretly, briefly,
like wasps' nests
gone papery in the attic.

The earths' satellite,
squalling baby, drains
the inlet morning, evening,
relentless. I cannot move
closer. I try

it on, not loving you,
slip an arm into it, sure,
what the hell. But
it's not right, something,
the length...

BOWLINE

The rabbit comes out of his hole,
goes around the tree,
stops stockstill, sniffing;
so far, the figure he's cut's
a question mark, a half-heart,
begging closure. Any scout
knows that, unfinished, that line
will pay past its cleat, useless
as pleading.

But sent down again, finished off,
the ending acquires utility,
becomes circuitous, fast,
the snag that hoists the rabbit
heavenward, jerking, while
the circle of disbelieving
scouts closes warily, staring
at the dilated eye, the quivering
figure in suspension, God's
handiwork arrested by a single

strand turned twice and
tightened, the staccato heart
eye-level, slowly bobbing in its snare.

RED RADISH

Give the seed 1/4 inch
of insults and stand aside.
In two days, they're lined up
in front of your car, loose
parade formation, snout-down
in the earth.
If the earth
has complaints, the radish
listens; if there's fire
in the mountain, he knows.
Untended, bolted, woody,
his pride's that no one
but the humans will eat him
(salt, please.)

The night my grandfather left,
he turned out his pockets
on the sinkboard: watchchain,
billfold, and a radish.
No one but me recognized his heart,
so dense and full of turpentine
that, above it, the rafters warped,
shakes parted, and he could
lie back and watch the constellations
wheel up.

RABBIT'S FOOT

Rear foot, real foot, strung
by a bootlace from Uncle Jack's Galaxie's
mirror, got him this far unshackled
and intact, he said. We couldn't touch it,
but while he was in the liquor store once
I studied and smelled it. Army buddy
from Youngstown's rabbit, gave Jack
the foot. He stroked it before
big games and dates. It didn't smell,
which surprised me.

Years later, dissecting a formaldehyde cat
in college, I thought of that foot, last thing
to leave the earth on that rabbit's
climax leap. Hadn't been enough
to save Jack, either; he'd dicked his way
around the world (my father liked to say,)
then'd been run over by a motorboat and
drowned right here in Chippewa Lake. I asked
his girlfriend Janine at the funeral
about that rabbit's foot, but
she was keeping it. It was all,
besides some pictures and cheap furniture
my grandma would be pried loose of.

ON A BREEZE THROUGH EUREKA

I admired his entry: disciplined, mature,
overarching clematis; so he snipped me
two quick cuttings as I left. Over the course
of our hasty summit, I brought him back
repeatedly, singlemindedly, to his Cleveland
boyhood with you; stories I'd heard too often,
but resuscitated, repopulated, recast;
he let me see you, briefly, with new eyes.

He saw you fall and fail. He saw you
screw up, scrape by, crash and burn and
bluster your way back, all things I was never,
in all my years in your house, allowed
to see. In the end, he told me one thing
no one else ever has: that we're alike,

and my heart stopped so long I actually
reeled, and never heard another thing he said
about rooting clematis. But it made it back,
half-dead, to my doorstoop, and now, ignored,
thrives. Each year it deepens, twisting further
up its porchside trellis, filling in more
of the blank squares obliging sky filled
brilliantly, for half my life, with hieroglyphics,
half-characters, towering, indecipherable nods.

THREE BACK TO BACK
BAD BACKS

1.

We were loading logs
on a Taiwanese register
when I see the boom jaws
open and logs start
bouncing down, slow
motion, kaBOOM. I

give a yip and go straight
over backwards, somersault
and light flatfoot
somehow in this half-
filled hold. Them

that saw it cheered.
But I've been out
of whack walking since.
Plus I can't stand to sit.

2.

Diagram:
Please shade in or indicate
areas where you feel, or have felt pain.

It's quack grass, cracked glass
warren and runs, spokes, hub,
witching branch, switching yard,
crabbed constellations; intermittent,
signifying, snaking radiations.
Here's where it starts and

where it marches, buttocks,
thighs, rhizomatous, bright, burning,
boring. My hands on that back
like a man in his half-

acre of corn, stalking
between new molehills,
pitchfork raised high above
the run, waiting for some sign,
for some bit of earth

to move.

3.

A lifetime of wiring wind
has planed back the willows
on this bluff, so that standing,
it feels like it's we who're
leaning forward, bent into some
terrific, straightening blow.

In Greece, in Santorini,
our first walk ended on your
apartment rooftop, overlooking
the world. We talked
about backs, beautiful backs, David's
back in Florence. And, hearing voices,
we bent and looked down

   a skewed airshaft, which earthquakes
   had shifted dizzingly out of plumb.
   You sneezed and grabbed your back.
   And there were open windows and tangled
   clotheslines and people shouting back
   and forth at each other through them.

ILWACO LIGHTHOUSE

for j.p.k.

We lay on our backs, mummy-bagged,
speeding, the steely light sweeping over
and over us, and recalled many things:
the donut shop we'd bike to mornings after
serving Mass, the Ford workers smoking there,
steaming the windows; your father's wall safe,
the dogeared pornography and three heavy pistols,
each carefully wrapped in an rag; your mother's mother
swearing at us in German over the blaring TV,
standing in the kitchen in her underwear, at midnight,
ironing. We had a night of it, and woke frosted,
high above the treacherous boat-eating, mile-wide
mouth of Columbia.
                    I didn't know then how stoned
you were, didn't know about the works taped up
under the dash, the trunkful of bloodied shirts.
You fucked up in Texas, you fucked up in Portland;
I found you a month later, trembling on your rooftop
on Glisan St., wondering how far down your rose
trellis went. You had more comprehending friends,
luckily, who knew which program you needed a ticket
to next.
        Now, when we meet, through I know
you haven't used in years, that easy draw
of memories, which colored me so vividly, feels
queered and distanced, like my hand's been stung
numb by nettles. We travelled so long in the same
direction, I never noticed where it was, exactly,
we veered apart. That thought chills me. What else
have I, impervious, missed? Was there a cry

for help? Did I miss it? Did the whole house seem
to you, just now, to move?

IN SERVICE

The paras are wheeling
into the gym, shouting insults
and greetings, sun slanting hard
off the dumbbells and parallel
bars. Last night,
in a movie, a beautiful
but pained artist was coming
unraveled, his creative life
slowly butchered by a drumbeat
of venal concerns, like food
and money. I would've liked

to believe it, but who's got
time? Here, I've got a roomful
of motorcycle wrecks, all young,
all angry, all with too-puny arms.
All, even the bitterest of them,
will eventually turn. Because
they can. Because it's there
in all of us, some gem-sized,
unwrapped, resuscitated coal
saying Stand up. Leave this.
Grasp the bars. Move forward.

AGAINST AMBITION

I've been watching your eyes wind their way
off the page, some daydream prizing them
away from the dazing, dense-looking text;
watching the irises, released, round
to a deeper focus, to the distance,
where tall trees, moss-backed, step forward
and back endlessly, in place, like zoo gorillas.
I know there is a place in you my love

hasn't reached; some tooth, some nuisance,
some never-made-right, deep-rooted. I remember
rifling, years ago, Gus' grandfather's boxed-up
medical texts, looking for clarification
on certain unverified points of female anatomy.
Instead, we came across pictures of tapeworms,
ten feet, captioned, coaxed painstakingly out
of their chloroformed hosts by slowly sliding

saucers of milk. We stared at that page
a long and skeptical time, tumbling reluctantly
to the possibility of such ravenous monsters
harbored unwittingly within. Let me slip
my hands inside your shirt for a moment; let me
feel the reciprocation, the smooth, unfamiliar
set of stops that another's heart always is.
Let me lead it, spilling and bitter, back

briefly into the world, the profoundly
unsatisfying world, where we rise anxious
every morning to alarms, and are arrested
moments later at a window by a simple glimpse
of water, the risen Sound, which regardless
of the narrow transit or the sky's stock stagings,
appears struck, stood up, made, by a thousand
glittering knifejabs, to speak.

SITTING UP WITH COLICKY COLE

If a yellow, field-colored rabbit springs straight
away from you in a beaten-down, rabbit-colored field,
sing out, watch him, dilated eye. Stitch that jittery
line into the quilt you make of the wetlands; recite it
to me when I'm rambling up Alaskan Way way too far
ahead of you, bent on business. Make ends meet,
yes, then look for the warren near rocks and ridges; never
corner a coon; never put more than three snakes together
in a dust-caked aquarium. Other than that, go. Harm none,
miss us. Bring us the details of who was flushed, and
how they startled and broke cover, wondering, as we do,
what in the wide world you are.

ORCAS BREACHING, TACOMA NARROWS

I'd seen the film in High School,
the humped waves travelling harmonically
from landfall to landfall, amplitude
rising, tossing cars and bridge parts far
down into the Sound. I wanted to see it
in person; Stanley wanted to fish. So

there we sat, with a rented tin boat and
an oil-rag sky when the monsters, glistening,
began to breach all around us, slamming
their bodies, slapping their tails,
tux-black and bright white, too huge, closing.

We later learned that the noise and show
spooked and schooled-up salmon, making
a tidier, denser meal for the pod;
we thought it was the Valkyrie song,
spectacular, thundering accompaniment

for our exit to the next world. I knew
myself, then, perhaps for the first time,
to be lucky; trouble life's flat water
thoughtlessly, and something enormous
comes corkscrewing, slow-motion, out,
smiling, mouth opening, showing its teeth.

DEAR PAT,

The pain I mean to give them,
taking the stoved, splinted fingers
in hand, is therapeutic, like the holes
Spanish Jesuits drilled dutifully
in the heads of heretics for a hundred
sorry years, praying the devilish ethers
might out. I close the swollen hand
in mine, talking; I talk about
my children, ask about theirs; I say
tell me if this becomes too much.

In San Paulo, Diane tells me,
campesinos coming out of her clinic
threw their pills in the dirt
and spat. They'd come a long, difficult
way expecting injections, something hard,
something sensational. Without toil,
they say, crops won't grow;
without pain, children aren't born.

I once hit a pig as hard as I could
between the eyes with my shovel
to keep him from biting at my boot
while I slopped his trough; it backed
him off two short, grudging steps.
He came again. I look them in the eye;
I say This is going to hurt; I say
This is the way, I must, I'm sorry.

GENEROSITY

The walruses were gliding, 3-ton and graceful,
he nudging her, backs dappled, on their slow meander
through the high-rise Mammal Wing tanks. And when
they rose, as if to joyful, unexpected music,
and began, turning face to face, to mate, she
with her back pressed flat against the glass, he
with his huge, reciprocating, otherworldly member,
you had just finished commenting on the unfitness
of men to shepherd children through such a demanding
instructional maze. If memory serves, that room
gradually filled with women mesmerized, struck mid-
step, still as pillars, in a blurred, oncoming sea
of whining and exhausted kids. To a one, those women
brooked questions calmly, answered soothingly,
but did not turn their faces away from the exhibition
climaxing, writhing and incandescent, before them.

When he turned again and wove indifferently away,
wry, sidelong looks were exchanged, very briefly,
among strangers. Then, spontaneously, and in near-
unison, they began cheering children forward, on
toward the exits and back up into the dazzling,
otherwise-undisturbed day.

SANDING MAPLE TABLE LEGS

My hand, this length, and the rhythm
are one; the edges broken, the cowlicks
and contradictions in the grain giving way
under the hot persistence of the rub.
For once, I'm happy to have it this way:
half-tranced, raw-fingered, the air a dusty
suspension cut more and more acutely
by a blade of afternoon sun. Two days, and
they're not quite glassy. I spit on them
once more.

      I must've dreamed my life
would turn out this way once, full of substantial,
finishable work that a signature wildness
showed through. Strangers, I imagined, might
stop, heads turned, and reach out compelled
to touch a corner, to caress.

              Now,
it's harder to say what it is I might want.
Today it's something with a likelihood
of outliving me; a table long and sturdy
enough to make love on, or corral the family
under when the rumbling, promised calamities come;
something we could do surgery on, or join hands
around, recombinant, grateful, and ceremoniously
mindful

      of silence, and the rise and fall
of our brief breath within it.

WILL THIS CHANGE?

It will,

I say, head up, eyes level, looking briefly
away from the bluish palm and cool, reattached,
stitch-riddled fingers I still hold up lightly
in my own. Nothing surer, I say simply,
thinking of the monkey grip I keep on my own
brittle gifts, and of the mangled flicker
I found on the shoulder of South Bay Rd.
last week, turning in tight circles and beating
his one wing furiously in the cinders.

I laid down my bike and stood and thought
a long time about killing him there,
his death a certainty, and all other
deaths seeming slower and somehow, surely,
more cruel. My devout Irish grandmother
taught me to shorten, always, wherever possible,
suffering's tenure. She was famous
for crushing and the mortally wounded
with large rocks and walking away.

She died herself suddenly, merciful god,
after living out her last years a showcase
of seizing, arthritic joints. She cursed
like a Teamster at each successive betrayal,
then wrapped her rosary around her hand
and prayed. I loved her, but couldn't listen
to that. Too, by then, I was out on my own,
seeing patients, seeing how inescapably
bodies, cruelly used, turn cruel. I told her

to walk. I told her to buy cut-up fryers,
for christsakes, before she murdered someone
with her wavering butcher knife, or fell
down dead stumping after her ancient, balding,
uncornerable hens.

About The Author

Timothy Kelly was born in Cleveland and educated at Oberlin, Boston University, and the University of Washington. Since 1982 he has worked as a physical therapist in Olympia, Washington, where he lives with his wife and two sons. *Articulation*, winner of the King County Arts Commission Publication Award, is his first full-length collection.